Easy Granola Bar Recipe

Design Your Own *Healthy* Granola Bars

With 13 kitchen tested no-bake recipe ideas to inspire you

A recipe template and collection

by Cheryl Hines

http://simplefrugal.com/contact

Easy Granola Bar Recipe

ISBN-13: 978-0615835846 (SimpleFrugal Publishing)
ISBN-10:0615835848

Table of Contents

Meet the Perfect Granola Bar…

You want a granola bar with just the right crunch and just the right chewiness. **Check**.

You can control *ingredients for your food sensitivities. Example: Make them without nuts, gluten-free, non-GMO, organic, etc.* **Check.**

You want one that doesn't have a lot oats, plenty of fruit (or no fruit at all), milk chocolate instead of dark, and a lot more nuts (or not)! **Check.**

You want a bar that you can stuff in your purse, your kid's lunchbox or take it backpacking. **Check.**

You don't want to heat up the oven to do it! **Check.**

And you want to "know" what's in the thing, too! **Double check!**

I wanted a bar like that too which is why I developed the **Easy Granola Bar Recipe.**

The recipe in reality is a *template*. Yes, I have included thirteen family recipes to inspire your own and get you started on your granola bar journey. But they are all based on the main template.

You see, once you learn how to prepare the sticky binder, you can add any possible combination of dry ingredients. Make it plain; make it fancy. More sweet, less sweet — even make them **gluten-free**, if need be. Have it your way!

This isn't your ordinary bland oat-filled bar… we are talking **gourmet**! Dare I say stellar?

A bit of history…

I am an incorrigible do-it-yourselfer! Since my large family loves granola bars, I just had to figure out how to make a bar that tasted better than those hard, dry, oat things that you buy in the store. Making my own bars kept the cost down as well.

So I began poking around my old recipe box and found one that sort of did the right thing but not quite. I did some major tweaking and LOTS of experimenting to come up with a template for the perfect no-bake granola bar.

The beauty of the recipe template is that it allows you to use just about any combination of sticky binder like honey, corn syrup, or rice syrup.

Then add your favorite blend of dried and crunchy things like oats (or not), rice cereal, pretzels, nuts and seeds, even ready-made trail mix or granola. Also, add coconut and dried fruit like raisins, cranberries, blueberries – you choose.

To make them extra special, you can add yummy things like chocolate, coffee, spices and flavors.

This way you can make a traditional granola bar with oats, nuts and seeds. Or try **Just Nuts**, an all nut version. Do you like white chocolate and cranberries? **Cranberry White Chocolate Bars** are the bomb! Or add in chocolate and coffee to make a "mocha" bar – see **Mocha Almond Crunch** or **Triple Chocolate**. Anyone love pralines? You have to try **Praline Crunch bars**. You are free to explore with this recipe.

I am excited to offer this "designer recipe" and hope you gain inspiration to make your own *perfect granola bar.*

Oh, and these are a no-bake bar, too. Thought you'd like that.

> ***Note to Purists: I have used corn syrup in some of my recipes. You certainly don't have to.***

So, just what is in this thing? Let's take a look!

The Basic Recipe Template

Makes 24 bars

Ingredients:

1 cup sticky binder
6 to 7 cups dry ingredients
Optional flavors and mix-ins

Equipment:

Medium sized heavy bottomed pan

Candy thermometer

Large bowl with wooden spoon

or

Bosch or Kitchen Aid with collar

Measuring spoons and cups

Cookie pan (lipped) or 13 x 9 pan

Pastry roller (optional but useful)

Pizza cutter (optional but useful)

Suggested sticky binder ingredients

Honey –This was our binder of choice for many years. Use honey when you want a sweeter bar. We now use a honey/corn syrup blend just below.

Honey/corn syrup blend – Sometimes honey's sweetness is overpowering. So to tone it down, I use a 50/50 blend.

Corn syrup - light or dark: Corn syrup is typically bland - not so sweet as honey. You can use non-HFCS Karo™ corn syrup instead of honey when don't want the strong honey taste. ***See article on corn syrup following this section***.

White, Brown Sugar, Sucanat™ – These can be added to change texture of the liquid sweeteners.

Molasses - typically you would use more honey or corn syrup and use molasses just to flavor it as in the Ginger Snap Bars.

Maple Syrup – I have used maple syrup but it will take more experimenting with it to get it right. I added corn syrup to keep it from "sugaring".

Rice syrup or agave – I have read that this works just like honey so try it if you like it.

Nut butters, like peanut or almond – here again, not a typical binder, per se, but it works best to **add nut butters to the syrup** stage before adding to the dry ingredients.

Marshmallows – yes, I seriously did add marshmallows as an option to the sticky part of this otherwise "healthy" recipe book. **See Marshmallow Dump Bars.**

A Word On Corn Syrup And High Fructose Corn Syrup

Perhaps you have heard about potential health risks in consuming fructose, particularly in HFCS (high fructose corn syrup). Since I have claimed that these are a healthy bar and you might question including corn syrup in many of these recipes, it seems appropriate to briefly talk about the difference between these sweeteners.

Corn syrup should not be confused with high fructose corn syrup. While both are derived from cornstarch, corn syrup (aka glucose syrup), is derived from a multi-step process which converts cornstarch into glucose. This is the corn syrup used in candy making for years. It is fairly bland and, as such, is suited to being flavored as in candy making. It is what I use in many of my recipes.

HFCS, on the other hand, takes this process several steps further which creates glucose/fructose syrup. Because of the fructose, it is sweeter than regular corn syrup, much like honey in sweetness. The food industry uses it widely because it is sweeter ounce for ounce than cane sugar or glucose syrup as it is the cheaper alternative to cane sugar. Thus it is in just about everything: sodas, condiments, baked goods, even spaghetti sauce.

You are the best judge as to whether you want to use the corn syrup in the recipes. Just know that it is different from high fructose corn syrup. Besides, you can easily swap out the Karo™ syrup for your own sticky sweetener.

Buyer Beware: Read the label! Karo bottles their corn syrup two ways: small glass jars or large plastic jugs. All my recipes use regular corn syrup, which comes in a smaller glass jar. But they also offer a corn syrup **blend** *which has HFCS (high fructose corn syrup) in it! It comes in the bigger half gallon jug. So read the label before buying.*

Suggested Dry Ingredients

Dry Ingredients

Oats – rolled or old fashioned work best.

Something Crunchy – Crispy rice cereal, Nutty Rice™, Chex™, hemp seed, bulk granola mixes, broken pretzels – anything you like to add a crunch to your bar.

Bulk trail mixes – I have included a recipe using trail mix

Almonds – Raw or roasted. We prefer almonds over peanuts, what can I say?

Peanuts – Raw or roasted.

Coconut – shredded or raw curls – I can't think of any bar *without* coconut.

Dried fruit – raisins, cranberries, cherries, acai, blueberries, etc. But keep in mind moist fruit will make the bars soggy pretty soon. So the drier the fruit the longer the bar will last.

Sunflower seeds – raw or roasted – if you like them.

Pumpkin seeds – another excellent choice.

Sesame seeds – raw or toasted. We like toasted for its rich, tangy bite.

Flax seeds & chia seeds – a popular addition that adds a nice lightly nutty taste.

Really – you can add anything. These are *your* bars – mix it up!

Optional Ingredients

Sea Salt – ½ to 1 teaspoon – adjust to taste. Particularly nice on the nutty versions. Use fine or coarse grind as you like it.

Butter or coconut oil – 1 to 2 tablespoons.

Vanilla, Orange or other extract – 1 to 2 teaspoons.

Cinnamon, ginger, other spices – adjust to taste.

Coffee – 1 to 2 Tablespoons regular or espresso grind.

Cocoa – 2 tablespoons.

Chocolate chips & other baking chips – milk chocolate, white chocolate, semisweet or dark chocolate; butterscotch chips or peanut butter chips – ½ cup or more of your choice of baking chips.

Please Read! General instructions

The cooking temperature in these instructions is for honey. See Notes On Cooking Temperature for how to cook the other sticky binder ingredients.

Note: All recipes are written for sea level. At higher elevations, please make appropriate temperature adjustments. See notes in Trouble Shooting section

1. Use a medium sized heavy bottomed sauce pan (one you would use to make candy in).

2. Add your honey and salt and bring to a boil over medium heat. Using a kitchen thermometer, bring temperature to 260°F (at sea level). Watch but no need to stir.

3. Meanwhile, combine your dry ingredients in large mixer bowl, like a Kitchen Aid or Bosch or just a large mixing bowl if doing it by hand.

   Exceptions: baking cocoa, spices, coffee, and smallest seeds – add them at step 5.

12

4. Place mixing collar on Bosch or Kitchen Aid (this keeps cereal from flying).

5. Once the honey has reached 260° F, remove the thermometer and remove pan from heat to a heat resistant surface.

   At this time, add flavors like butter, vanilla, cinnamon, coffee, cocoa powder as well as tiny seeds. Stir well. A whisk helps incorporate cocoa powder more smoothly.

6. Turn mixer on low speed and slowly pour syrup over all as it is mixing.

   -OR-

   you can **drizzle** syrup over dry ingredients, tossing and combining well using a wooden spoon. It helps to have a friend stir while you slowly pour (or vice versa).

7. Prepare a 13 x 9 inch pan or small cookie sheet (as in photos) using your choice of non stick spray or butter.

At this point, if you are adding chocolate or other baking chips, proceed to step 8.

If you are **not** adding chocolate, go to step 11.

Instructions for adding chocolate or other baking chips

8. Put roughly half the warm mixture in pan and pat it out by hand.

9. Next, evenly sprinkle the chocolate chips on.

10. Finally top this with the remaining granola mixture and press firmly into pan. The warm mixture will soften chips. Proceed to Step 12.

11. Dump warm granola mixture into pan. Spread evenly spread. Press out by hand.

12. Finish pressing using a pastry roller or rolling pin. This compacts the mixture to the perfect consistency.

13. **Cool before cutting into bars**. It really helps if the bars are room temperature to cut. If you try to cut while they are still warm, they just sort of "chase" the knife or cutter, especially if there are large nuts. Also, the chocolate gushes because it is melty.

Tip: If I am in a hurry, I will often cool the bars in the fridge for 5 to 10 minutes – longer if they have melty chocolate. Typically the hotter you cooked the syrup the shorter you need to chill before cutting. If the bars cool too long, they get too hard to cut. In which case you need to let them come up to room temp. You'll get to know how long to chill them.

14. **Cut into bars.** Cut them as you please. The Nutritional Facts are based on 24 bars so keep that in mind if you should choose to cut them differently.

    For 24 two inch square bars, cut 4 on the short side by 6 on the long side. For more traditional granola bar shape, cut 6 on the short side and 4 on the long side.

    A pizza cutter is perfect for this job. Use a knife for cutting that last bit where the pizza cutter doesn't quite reach.

15. **Important! Store in airtight container**, separating the layers with waxed paper. You can put bars in Ziplocs™ for individual servings. You can also wrap individual bars in foil or waxed paper but this is less desirable as the bar will get "sticky" the longer they are exposed to air.

Tips on adding baking chips or chocolate:

Chocolate or any kind of baking chip can be handled in various ways.

- "Sandwich" the chips between two layers of granola as I describe throughout this book. This is the least messy way to have chocolate and our preferred method.

- You can add baking chips during mixing. This will give a marbled effect but the bars may not hold together as well.

- You can layer the baking chips on top and warm them under the broiler till they are melty then spread to give an even layer of chocolate.

Notes on syrup cooking temperature

As a rule: the higher the temp, the harder the bar.

Cooking with just honey

Honey, though a natural product, is a fructose/glucose blend which is much sweeter than corn syrup. It also has flavor. I always use a light, clover honey although I have used orange blossom and alfalfa honey with great success. If you have access to your own honey, be aware the darker the honey the stronger the honey tastes.

It also cooks differently than typical candy cookery. Because it is a natural product, it can act inconsistently probably due to varying moisture levels as well as more or less fructose. When using honey I find that cooking to 260°F to 270°F gives the best texture. That is technically soft crack stage in candy making terminology.

Cooking with honey/corn syrup

Use this blend if you want to have a sweeter bar but not so sweet as a full honey bar. Use ½ cup honey and ½ cup corn syrup. Bring to 245°F to 250°F. Proceed as with honey instructions. This is my preferred "sticky".

Cooking with just corn syrup

For when you want a less sweet tasting bar. Use the same amount of corn syrup as you would honey. But you need to add 1 tablespoon of butter or coconut oil to help keep it pourable. Bring it to a boil over medium heat. Monitor temp to bring syrup to 240°F to 245°F (soft ball stage). Proceed as with honey instructions.

Troubleshooting & Cooking Tips

To cooks who live at higher elevations...

You'll need to make adjustment for your elevation. The rule of thumb is subtract 2°F for every 1000 feet above sea level. So if you are at 2000 feet above sea level, you cook honey to 256°F or corn syrup to 236°F.

For example, my niece lives in Bozeman, MT, so she has to reduce her honey temperature to 250°F. The first time she made the bars, she cooked her honey to 260° F which would be 10° F too hot at her elevation, so they turned out hard.

For more information on high altitude cooking, I found this useful article online: **http://aces.nmsu.edu/pubs/_e/E-215.pdf**.

This chart gives cooking temperatures based on the pamphlet above and my own findings:

Sweetener/temp	Sea level	2000' and above	5000' and above
Honey	260°F	256°F	250°F
Corn syrup	240°F	236°F	230°F
Honey/Corn Syrup	250°F	246°F	240°F

My bars taste too sweet – can I use less honey?

Remember that the recipe is a template and that you can tweak and adjust things. If you find the honey is too sweet, then use a blend of honey and corn syrup or just corn syrup alone. You might try blending honey and rice syrup. Feel free to "mess" with the ingredients but stick pretty close to the proportions: 1 cup sticky binder and 6 - 7 cups dry/crunchy.

My bars are turning out too hard – what am I doing wrong?

Quick Tip: To solve the immediate problem, leave your bars uncovered for a day or so and they will soften.

Your syrup is too "hard". In the future you can avoid this by making sure you don't go past the recommended candy temperature.

There are two reasons your candy temperature might be off. The first reason might be elevation, so refer to the above paragraphs.

Secondly, your candy thermometer might be "off". This involves calibration of your thermometer. To calibrate your candy thermometer, set it in a pan with water and bring it to a full boil and leave it in the boiling water for 5 minutes. It should register at 212°F at sea level. As noted above, as your elevation goes up, decrease boiling level by 1°F per 500 feet rise in elevation. If it reads higher or lower, note the difference and make adjustments to your recipe.

As an example, in Bozeman, MT the thermometer should register 202°F for boiling water.

Finally, believe it or not, even honey can have more or less sugar depending on how it was processed so it can get harder, too. This affects how hard the syrup is and will involve tweaking.

My bars are crumbly, not sticking together – am I doing something wrong?

Quick Tip: don't throw it away. Even "boo-boo" bars make great granola. Just add milk!

But the problem might be that you are adding too much fine/dry ingredients or not enough "sticky". You can increase the syrup or decrease the finer dry ingredients (think flax, chia, powdery ingredients like cocoa and quick oats). The finer the ingredients, the more surface area is exposed to the syrup giving a drier mix.

Or the syrup is too "hard" – see above.

My bars turned out sticky and won't hold together. I like my bars more crunchy – can I do that?

Of course. The trick here is to heat the honey syrup to the right temperature. See the notes on elevation and calibration above.

But if it doesn't turn out crunchy enough at first, you can bake the bars for 10 – 20 minutes or so at 325°F. This will continue to pull the moisture out of the granola. Cool briefly then cut.

If there is fruit or raw nuts in the mix, this will make the mix "soggy". For example if you used dates or apricots, they will make the mix sticky. Just make sure to cook the syrup longer next time. Fix as above.

My bars get all mushy on a hot day when they are still in the bag – how can I fix that?

As above, the quickest way to fix this is to heat the honey just a bit more to 265°F to 270°F. That makes the syrup harder when it cools. You can go as high as 290°F which is "brittle" stage. In our granola bar experiments we found honey has a "personality" and water/fructose/glucose can vary from one kind to another. You may need to test your honey with increasing or decreasing cooking temperature to achieve the right "chew".

As a general rule, the 260°F to 265°F for honey syrup (or 240°F for corn syrup) works for temperate climates but if you live somewhere where it is either typically hotter or cooler, you'll want to adjust the candy temperature up or down 5°F. The hotter the syrup, the harder the bar will be after it cools.

I have also found that as bars get warm, the fruit and raw nuts "sweat" and their moisture makes the bars wilt, too. Try to dry the nuts out more (by slowly baking or toasting them in oven) before combining. Fruit will dry out just by leaving package open for a few days.

I left my bars uncovered and now they are sticky – can I save them?

Like any candy, the more these bars are exposed to the moist air, the "stickier" they get. You can fix this by putting bars on an oiled sheet pan and bake them, slowly, for 10 to 20 minutes at 325°F.

Can I use rice syrup or agave instead of honey?

I have never tried to use rice syrup, but I have read around the Internet that you can. Just heat it like honey.

I am not sure about agave, though. And I had not seen anything on the net, either. But why not try it yourself? Then tell me about it so I can Include it in the next version.

Easy Granola Bar Recipe

Recipes to Inspire

The template is great if you are already familiar with flavors and textures. But what if you are new to granola bar cookery? Have no fear! I have included some of our most favorite combinations which we have experimented with and perfected over the years.

Get a feel for how the honey or corn syrup works by using one or more of the following recipes. Then go out on your own energy bar adventure! The whole point of this recipe template is to "mess" with them and come up with your own! My recipes may be too sweet for you. Don't let that put you off. Use corn syrup as it is less sweet.

Like your bars more chocolate-y? You decide how much to add. What if you don't have enough or don't even like coconut? So add more sunflower seeds or crispy rice. How about toasting the nuts and oats? Yes, it does make a nice difference in taste. To borrow a famous phrase:

Have it *your* way!

If you come up with a yummy combination, why not submit it at SimpleFrugal.com and I'll include it in the next version of this little collection.

Peanut Butter Crunch

24 bars

Our first rendition of the original recipe... pretty good we thought. But then we discovered we like whole nuts instead of nut butters. Try this one first then try the next ones that use whole nuts.

Ingredients

- 1 cup (240ml) honey (or corn syrup if you like your bars less sweet)
- ¾ cup (190g) peanut butter (or almond butter)
- 1 teaspoon vanilla (optional almond flavor for almond bars)
- ¼ teaspoon salt (¾ teaspoon salt for almond butter)
- 2 cups (200g) quick oats (can use old fashioned oats; just buzz them a bit in the food processor)
- 1 ½ cups (45g) crispy rice cereal
- ½ cup (50g) coconut, shredded
- ½ cup (50g) sunflower nuts
- 2 tablespoons sesame seeds
- 2/3 (120g) cup chocolate chips, optional

Instructions

In heavy saucepan, cook honey on medium heat till it boils. With a candy thermometer monitor honey till it reaches 250°F.

Meanwhile, combine dry ingredients in large mixer bowl. Put on collar if using mixer.

Once honey boils, add nut butter and cook for another minute till it begins to boil. Remove from heat.

While stirring constantly or with mixer on low, pour over dry ingredients and stir/toss to combine well.

Oil a 13 x 9 pan with spray.

Dump about ½ of the mixture and hand press evenly. Sprinkle with chocolate chips evenly over all. Top with remaining granola mixture. Press down well. Finish pressing with a pastry roller.

Cool and Cut! Read Step 13 & 14 in General Instructions.

Store bars in airtight container or zip seal bags.

Chewy, crunchy peanut butter in every bite. Yum!

ल্ডৰু

Nutrition Facts

serving size 1 bar

Calories – 177 | Calories from fat – 76 | Cholesterol 0g| Sodium 497mg | Potassium 125mg | Carbohydrates 23mg | Fiber 2.33g | Sugars 12.66g | Protein 3.5g

Praline Crunch Bar

24 bars

For you, Paulette. You pecan lovers have to try this! The butter makes these bars special.

Ingredients

    1 cup (120ml) light or dark corn syrup
    2 tablespoons butter
    ½ teaspoon salt
    2 cups (200g) oats
    1 cups (30g) crispy rice cereal
    2 cups (200g) pecans, chopped
    1 cup (100g) coconut

Instructions

In heavy saucepan, cook corn syrup, butter, and salt on medium heat till it boils. Using a candy thermometer, monitor boiling honey/syrup till it comes to 240°F.

Meanwhile, combine dry ingredients in large mixer bowl. Put on collar if using mixer.

Once honey/syrup reaches 240°F, remove from heat.

While stirring constantly or with mixer on low, pour over dry ingredients and stir/toss to combine well.

Oil or butter a 13 x 9 pan.

Dump the warm granola mixture into pan and hand press. Finish pressing with pastry roller.

Cool and Cut! Read Step 13 & 14 in General Instructions.

Store bars in airtight container or zip seal bags.

A delicate, lightly sweet bar packed with pecans!

☙❦❧

Nutrition Facts

serving size 1 bar

Calories – 157 | Calories from fat – 74 **| Total Fat 8.75g |** Sat Fat. 1.96g **|Cholesterol 2.54g|** Sodium 76.9mg **| Potassium 125mg |** Carbohydrates 20mg **| Fiber 1.83g |** Sugars 12.53g **| Protein 1.9g**

Mocha Almond Crunch

24 bars

For all you mocha lovers! This is deadly.

Ingredients

½ cup (120ml) honey
½ cup (120ml) corn syrup
½ teaspoon salt
2 tablespoon butter
2 tablespoons espresso or regular grind coffee
2 cups (200g) oats
2 cups (60g) crispy rice cereal
2 cups (300g) roasted almonds, chopped
2/3 cup (120g) chocolate chips, semisweet, dark or milk

Instructions

In heavy saucepan, cook honey/corn syrup, butter and salt on medium heat till it boils. Using a candy thermometer, monitor boiling honey till it comes to 250°F.

Meanwhile, combine dry ingredients in large mixer bowl. Put on collar if using mixer.

Once honey/syrup reaches 250°F, remove from heat and stir in coffee.

While stirring constantly or with mixer on low, slowly pour over dry ingredients and stir/toss to combine well.

Oil or butter a 13 x 9 pan.

Dump about ½ of the mixture and hand press evenly. Sprinkle with chocolate chips evenly over all. Top with remaining granola mixture. Press down well. Finish pressing with a pastry roller.

Cool and Cut! Read Step 13 & 14 in General Instructions.

Store bars in airtight container or zip seal bags.

Mocha Almond Crunch. I like regular grind coffee in mine – you can see the coffee!

☙❦❧

Nutrition Facts

serving size 1 bar

Calories – 165 | Calories from fat –65 | **Total Fat 7.83g** | Sat Fat. 3g | **Cholesterol 0g** | Sodium 63mg | **Potassium 107.4mg** | Carbohydrates 24mg | **Fiber 2.54g** | Sugars 12.53g | **Protein 3.18g**

Triple Chocolate Bars

24 bars

Triple Dark and plenty of chocolate! The roasted almonds make this super special.

Ingredients

½ cup (120ml) honey
½ cup (120ml) corn syrup
½ teaspoon salt
2 tablespoons cocoa
2 cups (200g) oats
2 cups (60g) Rice or Cocoa Krispies™
2 cups (300g) roasted almonds, chopped
1/3 cup (60g) white chocolate chips
1/3 cup (60g) chocolate chips, semisweet

Instructions

In heavy saucepan, cook honey/corn syrup and salt on medium heat till it boils. Using a candy thermometer, monitor boiling honey till it comes to 250°F.

Meanwhile, combine dry ingredients in large mixer bowl. Put on collar if using mixer.

Once honey/syrup reaches 250°F, remove from heat.

While stirring constantly or with mixer on low, pour over dry ingredients and stir/toss to combine well.

Oil or butter a 13 x 9 pan.

Dump about ½ of the mixture and hand press evenly. Sprinkle with chocolate chips evenly over all. Top with remaining granola mixture. Press down well. Finish pressing with a pastry roller.

Cool and Cut! Read Step 13 & 14 in General Instructions.

Store bars in airtight container or zip seal bags.

For you chocolate lovers... Triple Chocolate: cocoa powder, semi-sweet and white chocolate chips.

☙❧

Nutrition Facts

serving size 1 bar

Calories – 149 | Calories from fat –51 | **Total Fat 6.1g** | Sat Fat. 1.5g | **Cholesterol 0g** | Sodium 71mg | **Potassium 92mg** | Carbohydrates 23mg | **Fiber 2g** | Sugars 14.53g | **Protein 3.11g**

Just Nuts!

24 bars

Sometimes you feel like a nut! No cereals in this one. Naturally gluten-free! Very like the Kind™ bar.

Ingredients

- 1 cup (240ml) honey
- 1/4 cup (25g) of a combination of tiny seeds like sesame seeds, flax seeds, chia seeds, etc.
- ½ to 1 teaspoon sea salt (this is definitely adjustable if you like a saltier bar)
- 2 cups (300g) almonds
- 3/4 cup (75g) sunflower seeds
- 1 cup (100g) pumpkin seeds
- 1 cup (100g) coconut, shredded

Instructions

In heavy saucepan, cook honey on medium heat till it boils. Using a candy thermometer, monitor boiling honey till it comes to 270° F. This recipe calls for higher temp as there are no dry ingredients to stick it together.

Meanwhile, combine dry ingredients in large mixer bowl. Put on collar if using mixer.

Once honey/syrup reaches 270° F, remove from heat and stir in salt and flavors. I add the salt now instead of earlier because I like the taste of salt in this bar.

While stirring constantly or with mixer on low, pour over dry ingredients and stir/toss to combine well.

Oil or butter a 13 x 9 pan.

Dump warm granola mixture into pan and hand press evenly. Finish pressing with a pastry roller.

Cool and Cut! Read Step 13 & 14 in General Instructions.

Store bars in airtight container or zip seal bags.

Just Nuts! I think this bar is a beautiful mosaic of color and texture. Just a touch of coarse grind salt make these bars special.

෬෫

Nutrition Facts

serving size 1 bar

Calories – 140 | Calories from fat –62 | **Total Fat 7.4g** | Sat Fat. 1.5g | **Cholesterol 0g** | Sodium 141mg | **Potassium 134mg** | Carbohydrates 17.6mg | **Fiber 2.2g** | Sugars 13g | **Protein 3.1g**

Trail Mix Bar

24 bars

These have a good balance of fast carbs, slow carbs, and a touch of caffeine.

Ingredients

　　1 cup (240ml) corn syrup (see note below)
　　½ teaspoon sea salt
　　4 cups (200g) trail mix (Coastal Berry Blend is pictured)
　　2 cup (30g) Crispy rice cereal

Instructions

In heavy saucepan, cook syrup and salt on medium heat till it boils. Using a candy thermometer, monitor boiling syrup till it comes to 240°F.

Meanwhile, combine dry ingredients in large bowl.

Once syrup reaches 240°F, remove from heat.

While stirring constantly or with mixer on low, pour over dry ingredients and stir/toss to combine well.

Oil or butter a 13 x 9 pan.

Dump about ½ of the mixture and hand press evenly. Sprinkle with chocolate chips evenly over all. Top with remaining granola mixture. Press down well. Finish pressing with a pastry roller.

Cool and Cut! Read Step 13 & 14 in General Instructions.

Store bars in airtight container or zip seal bags.

Note: *I used plain corn syrup in this simply due to the fact that the trail mix I used had white yogurt chips in it which made it fairly sweet. The chips marbled into the bars so you cannot see them.*

Trail Mix Bar - this one made with Coastal Berry Blend and rice cereal – see the tiny wild huckleberries, cranberries, cashews, and almonds!

ଔଓ

Nutrition Facts

serving size 1 bar

Calories – 145 | Calories from fat –55 | **Total Fat 6.08g** | Sat Fat. 1.34g | **Cholesterol 0g** | Sodium 102mg | **Potassium 2.9mg** | Carbohydrates 21.45mg | **Fiber 1.3g** | Sugars 13.2g | **Protein 2.15g**

Cranberry White Chocolate Bars

24 bars

You will love these!

Ingredients

1 cup (240ml) honey (or corn syrup)
½ teaspoon salt
1 teaspoon lemon extract, optional
2 cups (200g) oats
1 cup (30g) crispy rice cereal
2 cups (300g) almonds, roughly chopped
1 cup (120g) Craisins™ dried cranberries
1 cup (100g) coconut
2/3 cup (120g) white chocolate chips

Instructions

In heavy saucepan, cook honey and salt on medium heat till it boils. Using a candy thermometer, monitor boiling honey/syrup till it comes to 260°F to 270°F (240°F for corn syrup).

Meanwhile, combine dry ingredients and cranberries in large mixer bowl. Put on collar if using mixer.

Once honey/syrup reaches 260°F to 270°F (or 240°F for corn syrup), remove from heat and stir in lemon flavor if adding.

While stirring constantly or with mixer on low, pour over dry ingredients and stir/toss to combine well.

Oil or butter a 13 x 9 pan.

Dump about ½ of the mixture and hand press evenly. Sprinkle with chocolate chips evenly over all. Top with remaining granola mixture. Press down well. Finish pressing with a pastry roller.

Cool and Cut! Read Step 13 & 14 in General Instructions.

Store bars in airtight container or zip seal bags.

The combination of tangy cranberries with the creamy white chocolate is – the bomb!

ೞ೮ಞಖ

Nutrition Facts

serving size 1 bar

Calories – 160 | Calories from fat –71 | **Total Fat 8.44g** | Sat Fat. 4g | **Cholesterol 0g** | Sodium 66.7mg | **Potassium 89mg** | Carbohydrates 221.57mg | **Fiber 1.79g** | Sugars 17.53g | **Protein 2.6g**

Liberty Bars

24 bars

Red, White and Blue and delicious, too! Take these on your next July 4th picnic.

Ingredients

1 cup (240ml) honey (or corn syrup)
½ teaspoon salt
2 cups (200g) oats
2 cups (60g) crispy rice cereal
1 cup (100g) coconut
½ cup (60g) blueberries
½ cup (60g) cranberries
2/3 cup (120g) white chocolate chips

Instructions

In heavy saucepan, cook honey or corn syrup and salt on medium heat till it boils. Using a candy thermometer, monitor boiling honey/syrup till it comes to 260°F to 270°F (240°F for corn syrup).

Meanwhile, combine dry ingredients, blueberries, and cranberries in large mixer bowl. Put on collar if using mixer.

Once honey/syrup reaches 260°F to 270°F (or 240°F for corn syrup), remove from heat.

While stirring constantly or with mixer on low, pour over dry ingredients and stir/toss to combine well.

Oil or butter a 13 x 9 pan.

Dump about ½ of the mixture and hand press evenly. Sprinkle with chocolate chips evenly over all. Top with remaining granola mixture. Press down well. Finish pressing with a pastry roller.

Cool and Cut! Read Step 13 & 14 in General Instructions.

Store bars in airtight container or zip seal bags.

Three cheers for the Red, White, and Blue: the Liberty Bar.

ᏮᏰᏬ

Nutrition Facts

serving size 1 bar

Calories – 139|Calories from fat –28**|Total Fat 3.25g|** Sat Fat. 2.35g**|Cholesterol 0g|**Sodium 75.56mg**|Potassium 47.4mg|**Carbohydrates 27.68mg**|Fiber 1.31g|**Sugars 20.3g**| Protein 1.63g**

Raw Power Bar

24 bars

As raw as you can get (well, the honey is cooked)!

Ingredients:

1 cup honey (240ml)
¼ - ½ teaspoon sea salt
2 cups (150g) raw almonds or peanuts, whole or roughly chopped
½ cup (50g) raw sunflower seeds
½ cup (50g) pumpkin seeds
1 cup (100g) coconut, raw
1 cup (60g) dates, pitted and chopped
½ cup (60g) cranberries

Instructions:

In heavy saucepan, cook honey and salt on medium heat till it boils. Using a candy thermometer, monitor boiling honey till it comes to 260°F to 270°F.

Meanwhile, combine dry ingredients in large mixer bowl. Put on collar if using mixer.

Once honey reaches 260°F to 270°F, remove from heat.

While stirring constantly or with mixer on low, pour over dry ingredients and stir/toss to combine well.

Oil or butter a 13 x 9 pan.

Dump warm granola mixture into pan and hand press. Finish pressing with a pastry roller.

Cool and Cut! Read Step 13 & 14 in General Instructions.

Store in airtight container or individual zips seal bags.

Raw Power! I pressed coconut onto these before they got hard.

ᏣᏗᏍᎣ

Nutrition Facts

serving size 1 bar

Calories – 168.9|Calories from fat –80|**Total Fat 9.53g**| Sat Fat. 1.67g|**Cholesterol 0g**|Sodium 93mg|**Potassium 151.4mg**|Carbohydrates 19.31mg|**Fiber 2.34g**|Sugars 13.79g|**Protein 4.28g**

Almond Bliss Bars

24 bars

I love Almond Joy™ candy bars. These are better!! Also, gluten-free when you use Nutty Rice™ instead of crispy rice cereal.

Ingredients

  ½ cup (120ml) honey
  ½ cup (120ml) corn syrup
  2 Tablespoon butter or coconut oil
  ½ teaspoon salt
  2 cups (450g) almonds, toasted and chopped
  1 cups (300g) coconut, curls or shreds
  1 cup (100g) oats
  2 cups (60g) crispy rice cereal (use Nutty Rice™ for gluten free bars)
  1 cup (180g) chocolate chips - you might like milk chocolate for this one!

Instructions

In heavy saucepan, cook corn syrup, butter, and salt on medium heat till it boils. Using a candy thermometer, monitor boiling honey till it comes to 250°F.

Meanwhile, combine dry ingredients in large mixer bowl. Put on collar if using mixer.

Once honey/syrup reaches 250°F, remove from heat and stir in any flavors.

While stirring constantly or with mixer on low, pour over dry ingredients and stir/toss to combine well.

Oil or butter a 13 x 9 pan.

Dump about ½ of the mixture and hand press. Sprinkle with chocolate chips evenly over all. Top with remaining granola mixture. Press down well. Finish pressing with a pastry roller.

Cool and Cut! Read Step 13 & 14 in General Instructions.

Store in airtight container or individual zips seal bags.

Almond Bliss: chunky almonds, large curls of coconut, LOTS of dark chocolate!

಄

Nutrition Facts

serving size 1 bar

Calories – 144 | Calories from fat –65 | **Total Fat 7.83g** | Sat Fat. 2g | **Cholesterol 2.54g** | Sodium 67mg | **Potassium 56mg** | Carbohydrates 19.7mg | **Fiber 1.67g** | Sugars 12.13g | **Protein 1.59g**

Ginger Snap Bars

24 bars

I love ginger snaps and molasses cookies so I had to make a bar that had those dark spicy elements. Image shows Supreme bar.

Ingredients

¾ cup (180ml) honey
¼ cup (60ml) molasses
½ teaspoon salt
1 tablespoon butter
1+ teaspoons ginger (adjust up or down to taste)
½ teaspoon cinnamon
¼ teaspoon cloves
3 cups (300g) oats
2 cups (200g) pecans, chopped
1 cup (30g) crispy rice cereal

Instructions

In heavy saucepan, cook honey and molasses and salt on medium heat till it boils. Using a candy thermometer, monitor boiling honey till it comes to 260°F.

Meanwhile, combine dry ingredients in large mixer bowl. Put on collar if using mixer.

Once honey/syrup reaches 260°F, remove from heat and stir in butter, ginger, cinnamon, and cloves.

While stirring constantly or with mixer on low, pour over dry ingredients and stir/toss to combine well.

Oil or butter a 13 x 9 pan.

Dump warm granola mixture into pan and hand press. Finish pressing with pastry roller.

If including chocolate chips dump about ½ of the mixture and hand press evenly. Sprinkle with chocolate chips evenly over all. Top with remaining granola mixture. Press down well. Finish pressing with a pastry roller.

Cool and Cut! Read Step 13 & 14 in General Instructions.

Store in airtight container or individual zips seal bags.

Ginger Snap Supreme! Made supreme with white chocolate and cranberries.

⊂⊃

Nutrition Facts

serving size 1 bar

Calories – 148|Calories from fat –61|**Total Fat 7.23g**| Sat Fat. 0.68g|**Cholesterol 0g**|Sodium 57.3mg|**Potassium 133.8mg**|Carbohydrates 20.6mg|**Fiber 1.96g**|Sugars 11.9g|**Protein 2.28g**

Marshmallow Dump Bars

24 bars

On a whim, I tried an old favorite with a twist – whatever cereal, nuts, or fruit I could find in the pantry and "dump" them in. You don't need rice cereal to make marshmallow treats.

Ingredients

3 tablespoons butter
3 cups (150g) mini marshmallows
6 cups (180g) combination of your favorite cereal, nuts, dried fruit
1 cup (150g) peanuts, dry roasted no salt
Coconut for dusting

Instructions

In a large pan, melt butter on medium heat. Add in marshmallows then stir and cook till melted. Cook a few minutes longer. It will look less like marshmallow cream and more like golden creamy syrup. (Marshmallows are gooey. This will make them more chewy and not so stringy.)

Take off heat. Stir in cereal, fruit, nuts and mix till well coated.

Dump mixture into buttered 13 x 9 pan and press out.

Cool and cut into bars. These are messy so once you cut them, press them into coconut or cocoa to make them easier to handle.

Note: I wasn't the first to try this twist but it is a fool proof way to make your own gourmet granola bars. I used Cheerios® and Chex® with nuts and chocolate chips.

If you use sweetened cereals, it can make this over the top sweet. Just sayin'.

Easy Granola Bar Recipe

Marshmallow Dump Bars pictured with chocolate chips

Nutrition Facts

serving size 1 bar (based on using rice cereal as the dry ingredients)

Calories – 93|Calories from fat –39|**Total Fat 4.6g**| Sat Fat. 1.36g|**Cholesterol 3.82g**|Sodium 40mg|**Potassium 49.4mg**|Carbohydrates 12mg|**Fiber 0.54g**|Sugars 4.71g| **Protein 2g**

The Original Granola Bar Recipe

24 bars

I got this recipe from a Mennonite friend. I have since seen this or similar recipes on the 'net. This recipe calls for peanut butter and uses brown sugar and corn syrup. It works OK. But I found it too sweet and the bars were not consistent - they often got crumbly. But here it is just so you can see the beginnings or the evolution of a perfect granola bar.

Ingredients:

½ cup (110g) brown sugar
½ cup (120ml) corn syrup
½ cup (85g) peanut butter
3 cups (300g) granola cereal
2 cups (60g) crispy rice cereal
½ cup (50g) chocolate chips

Instructions:

In a small sauce pan, mix brown sugar and corn syrup.

Bring to a boil over medium heat, stirring occasionally, until sugar is dissolved.

Meanwhile, put granola and rice cereal in a large bowl.

Remove from heat and immediately stir in peanut butter.

While stirring constantly or with mixer on low, pour over dry ingredients and stir/toss to combine well.

Add chocolate chips and stir well. They may get melty but that's OK.

Oil or butter a 13 x 9 pan.

Dump mixture into pan and press. You can use your hand, a jar or anything to press it firmly into pan. A pastry roller is perfect for this job.

Let this cool till firm.

Cool and Cut! Read Step 13 & 14 in General Instructions.

Store in airtight container. Keep bars separate by using waxed paper or foil between layers. Wrap each bar individually using zip lock bags.

ೞ೭ಎ

Nutrition Facts

serving size 1 bar

Calories – 132|Calories from fat –37**|Total Fat 4.48g|** Sat Fat. 1.33g**|Cholesterol 0g|**Sodium 43mg**|Potassium 80.4mg|**Carbohydrates 22mg**|Fiber 1.54g|**Sugars 10.71g**| Protein 2.98g**

Easy Granola Bar Recipe

Thanks so much…

for taking the plunge and sampling some of these recipes! I hope you have as much fun creating your own bars as we did.

Take a minute, if you would to leave a genuine review at Amazon. I *really* appreciate it.

If you feel something is missing or have some suggestions to improve this book, please go to the site, http://SimpleFrugal.com/contact and leave your questions or concerns. I'll get back to you ASAP.

Why not sign up to receive updates on this book too. Head on over to http://SimpleFrugal.com and sign up on my SimpleFrugal Family list and you will receive notification of when new books come out. I am always sending out goodies too.

Acknowledgements

So, no authentic recipe collection could come together without testers and tasters. Besides my kids and hubby Mark, I'd like to thank Linda Saffer, Darcy Saffer and Sarah Hines Saffer for testing these recipes in their own kitchens.

Special thanks to Paulette Hines for her honest input and sharp editorial eyes that made a good book GREAT!

Thanks, all, for making this book the best no-bake granola bar recipe collection on the market!

And thank you, God, for the inspiration in the first place.

Easy Granola Bar Recipe

Other books by SimpleFrugal Publishing

A Goldmine In Your Kitchen

"This is so delicious, I bet you could SELL it!"

Chances are you have thought about making and selling your own homemade goodies for profit.

Well, what's stopping you? You don't know how?

No more excuses because Cheryl Hines takes you step by step through the process of setting up and running a profitable home bakery. From inspiration to counting the cash, this book will show you how to do it all.

After three summers of making and selling out of her kitchen, Cheryl shares all her tricks and tips gleaned from firsthand experience. She tells you what mistakes to avoid to save blood, sweat and tears.

It is so much easier than you think to make and sell homemade baked goods you'll wonder why you didn't start sooner.

A Goldmine in Your Kitchen Recipes

Need inspiration for your home bakery business? Here are 25 proven money making recipes used by Hines Family Bakery.

This is the companion recipe book for **A Goldmine in Your Kitchen**.

Gluten-free Dark Chocolate Nutty Cups

Rich, Dark, Velvety - these mini tarts pack a wallop. These gluten-free treats resemble a creamy chocolate pie only they have no gluten, no dairy, no flour of any kind. They have a surprising ingredient which enhances the creaminess but doesn't take away from the overall scrumptiousness.

Easy Granola Bar Recipe

Printed in Great Britain
by Amazon

33698508R00034